D0816537

LIGHTNING BOLT BOOKS™

Inside the US Army

Jennifer Boothroyd

Lerner Publications • Minneapolis

For United States
Army families

Lerner Publications Company
A division of Lerner Publishing Group, Inc.
241 First Avenue North
Minneapolis, MN 55401 USA

For reading levels and more information, look up this title at www.lernerbooks.com.

Library of Congress Cataloging-in-Publication Data

Names: Boothroyd, Jennifer, 1972- author.
Title: Inside the US Army / Jennifer Boothroyd.
Description: Minneapolis : Lerner Publications, [2017] | Series: Lightning bolt books. US Armed
    Forces | Includes bibliographical references and index. | Audience: Grades K-3.
Identifiers: LCCN 2016038377 (print) | LCCN 2016039204 (ebook) | ISBN 9781512433913 (lb :
    alk. paper) | ISBN 9781512450675 (eb pdf)
Subjects: LCSH: United States. Army—Juvenile literature.
Classification: LCC UA25 .B595 2017 (print) | LCC UA25 (ebook) | DDC 355.00973—dc23

LC record available at https://lccn.loc.gov/2016038377

Manufactured in the United States of America
1-42027-23897-10/12/2016

Table of Contents

What is the US Army?

The US Army is one part of the US military. The army handles land combat. It is also in charge of defense.

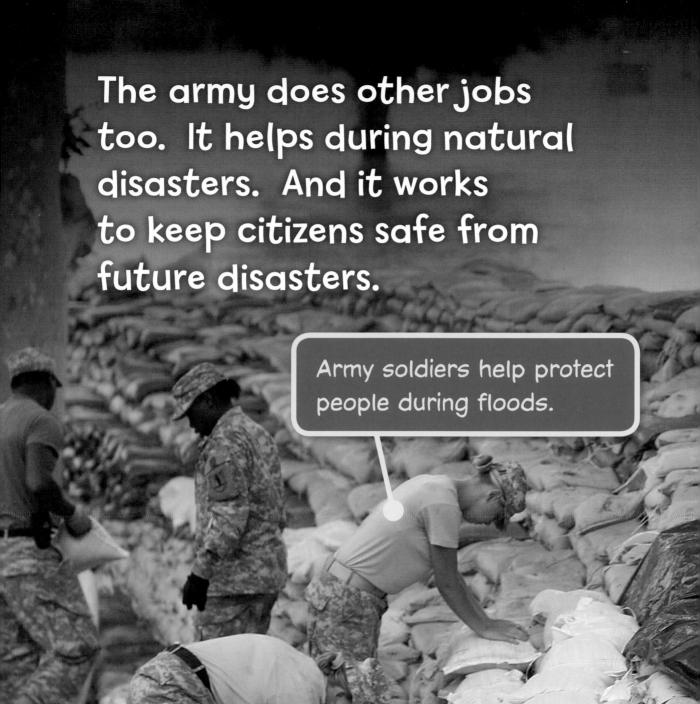

The army does other jobs too. It helps during natural disasters. And it works to keep citizens safe from future disasters.

Army soldiers help protect people during floods.

US Army bases are in many states across the country. They are also in other countries.

Camp Humphreys is a US base in South Korea.

Some kids go to school on the base. Soldiers posted on the base sometimes speak to classes or at school events.

A base is like a neighborhood. It has places to live and work. It has stores and places to have fun, such as bowling alleys.

Army Training

Men and women who want to join the army must pass Basic Combat Training. Recruits learn the skills needed to be a good soldier.

A recruit is someone training to become a soldier.

Soldiers must
be physically fit.

Recruits train for ten weeks
at one of four army bases
in the country. They attend
classes and spend many
hours a day exercising.

Soldiers in the army need many combat skills. Recruits learn to fight with their bodies and to use different weapons.

A gas mask keeps harmful gas away from a person's face.

The tear gas chamber is one of the toughest parts of training. Recruits enter a room filled with tear gas while wearing gas masks.

The recruits are ordered to remove their masks. The gas makes their eyes water. It makes it hard to take deep breaths. The recruits must stay until they're ordered to leave.

This training tests recruits' bravery, toughness, and ability to follow orders.

This soldier collects a fuel sample as part of training for delivering fuel and water to other soldiers.

After basic training, soldiers train for their special job in the army.

Army Equipment

The army uses a variety of equipment. Some soldiers have to carry a lot of equipment to do their jobs.

The army has different types of armored vehicles. They carry weapons used in battle. These vehicles protect the soldiers inside.

Helicopters are very useful in the army. They move fast and can land almost anywhere. They can carry soldiers and equipment. Some can even launch missiles.

The Army of the Future

The army is always studying new ideas to keep its soldiers and the country safe. Robots could rescue wounded soldiers. Hoverbikes could keep soldiers away from enemies on the ground.

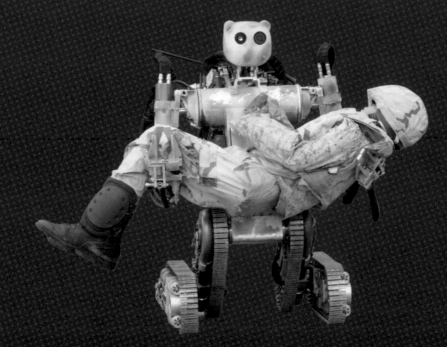

Cyberattacks are attempts to damage or destroy a computer network.

The army will count on computer technology even more in the future. New programs will need to be developed to prevent cyberattacks.

The US Army works hard to keep our country safe now and in the future.

Infantry Soldier Gear Diagram

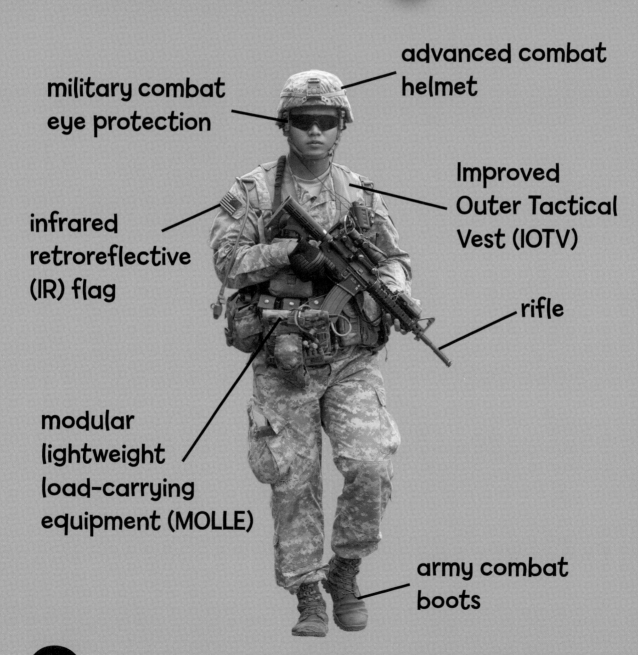

advanced combat helmet

military combat eye protection

Improved Outer Tactical Vest (IOTV)

infrared retroreflective (IR) flag

rifle

modular lightweight load-carrying equipment (MOLLE)

army combat boots

US Army History

- The US Army was created on June 14, 1775. Its goal was to fight the British army during the American Revolution (1775-1783).

- People volunteer to join the army. Sometimes the US government requires people to join the army. This is called the draft. The last drawing for the draft was in 1975.

- Women were first allowed into the regular army in 1978. But they were not permitted to have certain jobs, especially in combat. Since 2016, women can serve in any job in the US Army.

Glossary

combat: fighting in a war

cyberattack: an attempt to damage or destroy a computer network

defense: the act of defending someone or something from attack

missile: a weapon shot through the air

natural disaster: an event such as a forest fire, earthquake, tornado, or flood that causes damage

recruit: a person training to join the military

soldier: a member of the army

Further Reading

About the Army
http://www.goarmy.com/about.html

Kohl, Peter. *My Dad Is in the Army*. New York: PowerKids, 2016.

Lusted, Marcia Amidon. *Army Rangers: Elite Operations*. Minneapolis: Lerner Publications, 2014.

Silverman, Buffy. *How Do Tanks Work?* Minneapolis: Lerner Publications, 2016.

U.S. Army Symbols & Insignia
https://www.army.mil/symbols/index.html

Zuehlke, Jeffrey. *Helicopters on the Move*. Minneapolis: Lerner Publications, 2011.

Index

Photo Acknowledgments

The images in this book are used with the permission of: US Army/SSG Britney Hiatt, p. 2; US Army/Spc. Kyle Edwards, p. 4; © Joe Raedle/Getty Images, p. 5; US Army/Sgt. Christopher Dennis, p. 6; US Army/Spc. Nicholas Holmes, p. 7; US Army/Spc. John Onuoha, p. 8; US Army/ Sgt. 1st Class Brian Hamilton, pp. 9, 23; US Army/Sgt. Javier Amador, p. 10; US Army/Staff Sgt. Ronald Shaw Jr., pp. 11, 12; US Army/Sgt. 1st Class Walter Talens, p. 13; US Air National Guard/Tech. Sgt. Sarah Mattison, p. 14; US Army/Sgt. Todd Robinson, p. 15; US Army/Capt. Brian Harris, p. 16; TATRC via US Army, p. 17; US Army/Sgt. Marcus Floyd, p. 18; US Army/Sgt. Jon Heinrich, p. 19; US Air Force/Staff Sgt. Christopher Hubenthal, p. 20.

Cover: US Army/Spc. Nathaniel Nichols.

Main body text set in Billy Infant regular 28/36. Typeface provided by SparkType.